Monet

A Visit to Giverny

Text by Françoise Bayle

preface by Florence Van der Kemp

*"One must absolutely
make a pilgrimage to Giverny,
to this flowered-sanctuary,
to have a better understanding of the master,
a better grasp of the sources
of his inspiration and to imagine him
still alive among us."*

Gerald Van der Kemp

Preface

The History of a Renaissance
Homage to Gerald Van der Kamp

After the death of Claude Monet, his son Michel inherited his legacy and thus Giverny. However he didn't settle there; it was Blanche, Monet's daughter-in-law who looked after the painter until his death, who attended to the estate. When she in turn died in 1947 the garden was gradually neglected, Monet's paintings were sold and the house was no longer really maintained.

On 19 January 1966 Michel Monet was killed in a car accident on his way back to Giverny. In his will he bequeathed the whole estate to the Academy of Beaux Arts, who appointed architect academician Jacques Carlu as curator of the house. Mr. Carlu ordered that work be started on the house urgently. He began by restoring the roof which was in very poor state, by installing the 46 paintings of Monet, left by his son, in the Marmottan Museum, and had the very deteriorated Japanese prints put away. Through lack of credit however, the house was left without heating and the furniture, the paneling, the floors and stairs suffered terribly from the humidity. It was the same for the second studio and for the studio of the Nympheas, which had begun to be overrun by vegetation.

In 1977 Gerald Van der Kemp, my husband, was appointed curator of Giverny by his colleagues at the Academy of Beaux Arts. He immediately undertook the restoration of the property, beginning with the gardens. He hired a head gardener, Mr. Gilbert Vahe, a former student of the National School of Horticulture, and surrounded himself with several competent advisors: Mr. Andre de Vilmorin and Mr. Andre Devillers, who, having had often come to Giverny with Georges Truffaut, told him, assisted by Mr. Thibaudin, of his experience and memories. Lastly, he benefited from Mr. Toulgouat's, Monet's great-great-nephew, and his wife's specialized studies in the theoretical reconstitution of gardens. Thanks to a credit from the Institute and a grant from the departmental council of the Eure region, from the prefecture of the Eure and from the company, Richesses, in the Eure, work was started. When funds ran short we decided to turn to the United States, that we know well, as I preside over the Versailles Foundation which helped so much in the restoration of the Versailles domaine. This foundation was thus authorized to receive the innumerable donations from Americans who love Giverny and the work of Claude Monet. Some of them were extremely generous. Thanks to the donation of Lila Acheson Wallace and to the invaluable advice of the devoted Georges Luquiens, the architect of the Institute, the restoration of all the buildings was undertaken: the façade, the dining room, the kitchen, the living room-studio, and the bedrooms upstairs. Soon, thanks to the generosity of the ambassador, Walter Annenberg, a tunnel gave visitors direct access to the water garden. As for the studio of the *Nympheas*, two large donations from Mr. and Ms Michel David-Weill permitted its restoration at great expense.

Under the passionate and attentive eye of Gerald Van der Kemp, Giverny slowly regained its former luster, to become henceforth like days gone by, under the benevolent shadow of the master.

May this guide give visitors the feeling of walking in the footsteps of the great painter who so loved this house and garden.

Florence Van der Kemp

Monet

Giverny

Biography

The House

The Clos Normand

The Water Garden

The Studios

The Foundation

Direction of the Visit **>**

Visit to Giverny

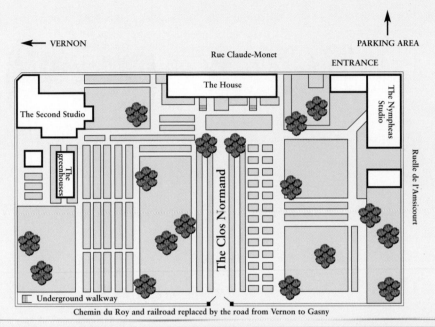

← VERNON

PARKING AREA

Rue Claude-Monet

ENTRANCE

The House

The Second Studio

The Nympheas Studio

The greenhouses

The Clos Normand

Ruelle de l'Amsicourt

▥ Underground walkway

Chemin du Roy and railroad replaced by the road from Vernon to Gasny

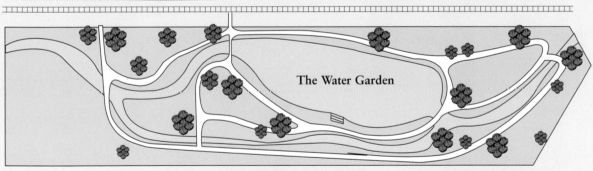

The Water Garden

"When I say that Claude Monet was born
in Paris on rue Lafitte, that is,
in the quarter of art dealers – a possible sign
of predestination –, I won't be saying very much.
If I add, however, that he spent his whole childhood
in Le Havre, and there, enamoured with the movements
of light that the tumultuous ocean on coasts
receives from the infinite space,
perhaps that will explain this familiarity of the eye
with the luminous gymnastics
of a wildly fluctuating atmosphere
which throws all the nuances of all the tones
to waste in the wind and waves."

Clemenceau

Biography

Monet was born in Paris on 14 November 1840, two days after Rodin. He wasn't a Parisian for long since his parents moved to Le Havre when he was five years old. It was there that he discovered the countryside and the sea. When he was very young he sketched caricatures of close relations and also drew seascapes and boats. Soon he met Boudin who convinced him to give up his caricatures and go and paint with him outdoors. "Boudin, with his inexhaustible goodness, undertook my education. My eyes eventually opened and I understood nature; at the same time I learned to love it".

After attending the Swiss Academy in Paris and once he was back from Algeria where he had voluntarily joined the military service, he met another painter, Jongkind, in Paris during the summer of 1862. They worked together outdoors in Honfleur, Sainte-Adresse and the surrounding areas where Monet would often return afterwards. In the autumn he entered the Gleyre studio in Paris, and there he met other artists who would become his close friends: Renoir, Sisley and Bazille.

During all the years which preceded his settling down in Giverny Monet stayed in Paris on occasion, but most often he painted in the areas surrounding his successive holiday resorts, Ville-d'Avray, Bougival, Argenteuil, Vetheuil, and Poissy, together with, from time to time, his new painter friends: the great Bazille, who died very young in combat in 1870, Renoir and Manet. Already Monet's appreciation for landscapes was manifest: when he set his easel up next to Renoir, he was much more interested in nature, water and light than he was in figures.

It was also during this period that, weary of being more often than not refused by the Salon, Monet and his friends, soon to be described as impressionists, decided to organize independent exhibitions. The first took place from 15 April to 15 Mai 1874: it brought together the paintings of Boudin, Degas, Guillaumin, Morisot, Cezanne, Renoir, Monet... and provoked sarcasm and criticism. Other exhibitions followed; there were eight in all, the last being in 1886. The times were hard for most artists and Monet didn't escape financial difficulties, even if certain friends, Bazille and Caillebotte, who were better off, helped him regularly.

"Apart from painting and gardening, I'm not good at anything." Monet

"I'm in rapture; Giverny is a marvellous home for me." Monet to Duret

Monet and Gustave Geffroy
photographied by Sacha Guitry

Another individual, an art dealer named Durand-Ruel, lent him money several times and began organizing private exhibitions for him; the first was in June 1880. From then on Monet tended to be independent of his former impressionist friends and participated only now and then in their exhibitions.

In 1876 Ernest and Alice Hoschede commissioned Monet for their chateau in Montgeron and the two families became friends. The Hoschede's affairs, However, things weren't going well for the Hoschedes: Ernest's absences were more and more frequent and Madame Hoschede and her six children ended up moving in with Monet in Vetheuil in the summer of 1878.

On 5 September 1879, when Monet lost his wife Camille, Alice gave the education of Monet's two young sons as a pretext for staying in Vetheuil. In December 1881 the Hoschedes and the Monets moved into a house in Poissy, where Monet wasn't very happy; he spoke of the awful Poissy. The lease on the house fell due in April, 1883.

The painter, 43 years old, then set out to find a permanent place to live that pleased him. He went all over the valley of the river Epte, which was in the region of Vernon that he already knew, as several years before he had stayed in Vetheuil. He found a house to his liking, *Le Pressoir* (The (fruit) press-house) in a little village called Giverny, in the Eure region.

He resided first there firstly as a tenant and it was during the days of settling in that he learned of the death of another painter and a very close friend, Manet. He moved in with his two children, Madame Hoschede and her six children: the house was big, only about 70 kilometres from Paris, was near a little town where the children could get a suitable education, had a garden and he knew well the quality of the light which bathed the landscapes of the region. Monet was perhaps, of all the impressionists, the most sensitive to contact with the outdoors and to the rendering of light.

At Giverny, where he would spend the second half of his life, Monet devoted himself to his painting, his garden and his family, or rather his two families. It was only in 1892, one year after the death of Ernest Hoschede, that he married Alice, thus putting an end to an ambiguous situation. Though very quickly attached to Giverny, he travelled regularly to discover new landscapes in a different light as sources of inspiration: from the Mediterranean to Norway, passing through Holland, from Belle-Isle to Creuse, from London to Venice, and always to the Normandy coast which he was so fond of. The letters he sent to his close friends and family revealed his homesickness more than once.

When he was at Giverny, he led an industrious and well-ordered life. Dressed in a three-piece suit made of a coarse herringbone fabric or of linen, a batiste shirt with pleated cuffs which jutted out of his jacket sleeves, he sported a beautiful, natural beard and an eternal cigarette which he never finished. He woke up early, sometimes very early, and didn't stay up late, even if the evenings were sometimes occupied with walks in the garden or games: outside games like parties of croquet, ninepins, or cup-and-ball game or inside games like cards, draughts or backgammon. In the evening, especially in winter, he greatly enjoyed reading, often aloud: the Goncourt, Mirbeau, Ibsen, Maeterlinck, Flaubert, Zola, Tolstoy, Jules Renard, Michelet's *History of France*, the *Memoires* of Saint Simon, and the *Journal* of Delacroix. During the summer, the rattan armchairs from the studio-living room were taken outside and everyone sat around to chat.

Monet was rigourous about mealtimes and they were served at 11:30 and at 19:30. According to Jean-Pierre Hoschede, a bell was rung twice to call everyone and Monet even blew a whistle for those who were further away. He appreciated wine and good food, with the occasional odd thing: the asparagus had to be barely cooked, thus two sittings were required, the salad was abundantly seasoned with crushed pepper-corns, cooking salt, a lot of olive oil and a little wine vinegar, the wings of the duck were put back on the grill after being heavily sprinkled with the same pepper, cooking salt and nutmeg. He loved lobster, for which he concocted his own sauce with a base of crushed pepper-corns again and cream obtained from the shell, but also game and especially woodcock. After a coffee, he wouldn't refuse a small glass of plum brandy.

He accepted to organize Sunday walks with the family, after lunch or excursions for the day or longer by car or by train. There were numerous pretexts: to taste the famous tart at the Hotel Tatin in Lamotte-Beuvron, in the Loir-en-Cher, to see the tidal bore at Caudebec-en-Caux, or to simply discover or see again some beautiful landscapes. He even went as far as to attend a few car races, making the front page of certain magazines with his family. In nice weather he played tennis on an improvised court and he bathed almost everyday with the children; the roof of the boat-studio served as a divivig board for everyone to dive. Though he disregarded the bicycle, the telephone, the radio or the phonograph, and he wasn't interested in either photography or cinema, he did have electricity put in the house as soon as it was installed in the village and he purchased a car in 1900, a Panhard, for which he hired a chauffeur, who also served as a mechanic.

If Monet was certainly not a city dweller, he wasn't a country fellow either and contrary to what is sometimes said, he regularly left his dear Giverny to go to Paris, at least as long as Alice was alive. There he went to concerts where he heard the famous base-baritone Chaliapine and to the theatre where he attended the first plays of his friend Mirbeau. He also went to wrestling matches and dined with his many friends; in the 1890's, he went to the Impressionists' dinners at the Café Riche where he saw his former friends and other companions almost once a month. While Monet had rather a cheerful disposition, he had fits of anger when his work wasn't going as he wished. Then he would abandon his paintings; when he didn't destroy them,

"Ah! Gentlemen, I'm afraid I don't receive visitors while I'm working. If I am interrupted while I'm working it wears me out and I'm lost. It's easy to understand that I'm running after a slice of colour."
Monet to Georges Bernheim and Rene Gimpel

he would pile them up against the wall in his studio. Exept for a few still lifes, bouquets or portraits, Monet, like his impressionist friends, painted his landscapes out of doors and didn't hesitate to tirelessly rework them there. It was when he was living in Giverny that he did his famous series, at the price sometimes of a certain distance: *Haystacks* during the summer of 1890 and then *Poplar Trees*, the *Cathedrals of Rouen*, *Mornings on the Seine*, and *Views of the Thames*. He would install himself in front of his easel, often standing, with a small folding tripod to sit on, and a big parasol ready to shelter him when the sun was too strong. When he was at work, it was better not to disturb him: the subject wouldn't wait, the light was fleeting and vibratile. His eyes went from the subject to the canvas, from the subject to the palette, from the palette to the canvas, and only a cigarette to light barely interrupted the comings and goings. Then, once back at the studio, Monet often resumed his work, sometimes working away at it furiously, as if in persisting with the material he could express the essence, the time stopped and an instant of light, before signing it. It was only when he was older that, wishing to paint very big formats on the theme of water lilies, he did his *Big Decorations of Nympheas*.

Many of his friends came to visit him: painters such as Renoir, Cezanne, Caillebotte, Pissarro, Mary Cassatt, Berthe Morisot, Sargent, Roussel, Vuillard, Bonnard, Signac, and Luce but also men of letters, musicians, sculptors, politicians such as Geffroy, Mirbeau, Rodin, Valery,

Sacha Guitry, Chabrier, the singer Faure, Maupassant, Clemenceau, and Thadee Natanson and of course more and more art dealers with time such as Durand-Ruel, the oldest, a friend and patron from the beginning, Josse and Gaston Bernheim, and Rene Gimpel. Monet was successful at the time of Giverny, both in France and abroad where henceforth numerous exhibitions would be organized. At the end of his life, in spite of the cataract that he only decided to have operated on in 1923, Monet continued to work relentlessly, particularly on the *Big Decorations of Nympheas*. Monet was a widower for several years, and it was his daughter-in-law Blanche, the daughter of Alice and the widow of John, one of Monet's two sons who died in 1914, who watched over him until he died on 5 December 1926, at the age of eighty-six. In respect of his last wishes only a few friends and close family were present at his funeral: Roussel, Vuillard, Bonnard, Thadee Natanson, and Clemenceau, his dear friend who waited for the funeral procession at the cemetery.

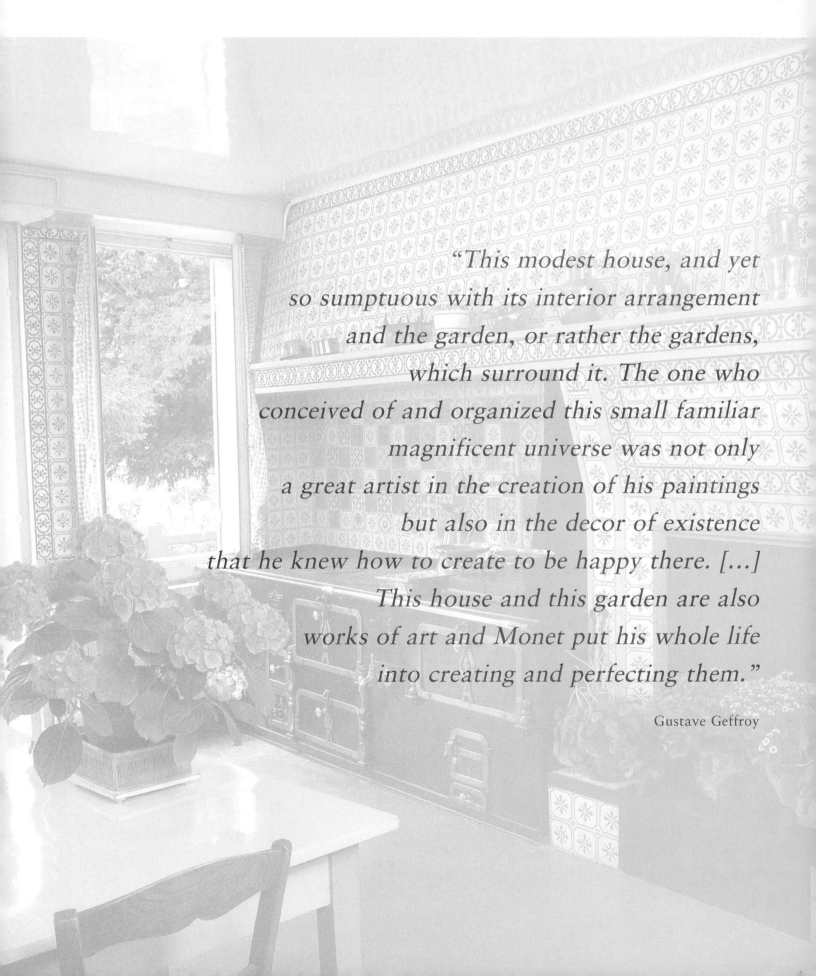

"This modest house, and yet
so sumptuous with its interior arrangement
and the garden, or rather the gardens,
which surround it. The one who
conceived of and organized this small familiar
magnificent universe was not only
a great artist in the creation of his paintings
but also in the decor of existence
that he knew how to create to be happy there. [...]
This house and this garden are also
works of art and Monet put his whole life
into creating and perfecting them."

Gustave Geffroy

The Giverny House

The house that Monet bought was a rather large impressive house that he adopted immediately. "It's hard for me to leave Giverny, especially now that I have arranged the house and garden to my taste," Monet admitted to Mallarme only a few months after acquiring Giverny.

This house appeared shorter then: the two ends, east and west, were still only one level barns on a beaten earth floor. Already roughcast in pink, it had gray shutters that would soon be painted a bright green, like the doors and the large balcony which ran across practically the whole facade and which permitted direct entry to the rooms from the ground floor. It was Monet who had this terrace built lengthwise, removing the small stone stairs. Virginia creeper plants and rose bushes would soon climb all over the house.

To the left of the entrance is the little reading room, whose walls and furniture are painted in two tones of blue; it opens onto a little vestibule through which one has access to the rooms that Monet built on the site of a little barn adjoining the house. On the ground floor a studio with varnished floor and paneling, where big windows let light enter, occupies the space of the old barn. It was here that Monet worked until the beginning of 1899, when he had a second studio built in a separate building. The "first" studio was then transformed little by little into a living room where it was the custom to have coffee and brandy after lunch, making it a "living room-studio." Rattan chairs, sofas, rugs, an easel, writing desks, photos and familiar objects impart an intimate and comfortable atmosphere. On the walls equipped with a system of small wood rulers, the painter hung his paintings in three rows.

In coming out of the studio and going up the small staircase in the hall there are two very bright rooms built on the first floor, just above the studio, forming Monet's apartments. His bedroom still has his 18th century inlaid desk and an old chest of drawers while the walls and the armchairs have regained their fabric of the past. Monet, who had acquired a beautiful collection of paintings, particularly from his painter friends, had arranged it in his bedroom and in the adjoining rooms.

An exceptional collection said Jean-Pierre Hoschede, Monet's son-in-law, since it was in the company of "a Corot, four Jongkind, three Delacroix, a Fantin-Latour, a Degas, two Caillebotte, three Pissarro, a Sisley, twelve Cezanne, of which *The Negro*, nine Renoir, of which the *Portrait of Monet Reading* and that of Madame Monet and also *The Kasbah* [...], five Berthe Morisot of which the *Young Girl and the Greyhound*, a watercolour of Cheret and two of Signac, a pastel of Vuillard and two bronzes of Rodin." After Monet's apartments are those of Alice, also made up of a bathroom and a bedroom. All the rooms open largely onto the garden. Beyond the central staircase are the children's bedrooms and above, in the attic are the staff's quarters. After coming back down the central staircase, one enters, beyond the entrance, a spacious dining room because, in fact, it had formerly been a bedroom and a kitchen. Monet had the walls, the ceiling, the windows, the doors, the chairs, the two buffets and the sideboards painted in two tons of yellow, one rather pale

and the other deeper. In the centre of the room is a large table, yellow too, which can seat up to fifteen guests. "Bleus de Chine", porcelain from Limoges and curtains create the warm atmosphere evoked by so many visitors. There are no paintings on the walls, only prints of famous Japanese artists such as Hokusai, Hiroshige and Utamaro are all over, even on the doors and in other rooms of the house like the little blue living room, Alice's apartments, the corridors... It appears that Monet discovered and acquired his first prints during a stay in Zaandam in Holland in 1871. Upon his return to Paris he continued to purchase them from a few art dealers, particularly at Bing's and at the Japanese Hayashi's: in his journal, dated 17 February 1892, Edmond de Goncourt noted that he had run into Monet "often at Bing's in the little attic of Japanese prints", and Blanche, Monet's daughter-in-law recalled the regular visits to Giverny of the Japanese art dealer who had even exchanged prints for two paintings of the master.

A door leads to the kitchen which was built, like the living room-studio, on the site of a little adjoining barn. Its blue and white earthenware, its magnificent oven, its copper utensils, and its stone sink conjure up the bustle which must have reigned when the eight children of Monet and Alice had to be fed but with their numerous guests too, who all talked about the excellent food served at Giverny; certain guests were real regular visitors like Clemenceau, Mirbeau, Geffroy or Renoir.

"What I think about Giverny in this beautiful weather and how I envy you being there, you can't imagine, but I'm a prisoner and I must go right to the end, even though in reality I have almost no strength left, it's exhausting, and I'm working with a feverish ardor." Monet to Alice

"*I'm still waiting for your promised visit. Now's the time; you'll see a magnificent garden but you'll have to hurry […]. Later on, all the flowers will be gone. Arrange it with Geffroy and write to me. I'm counting on you. Moreover, I have loads of new paintings. With my best wishes. Give Geffroy a shake and come.*"
Monet to Clemenceau

"This living room-studio was full of life and youth in the days of 1886 when I went there for the first time: young girls, young people, adolescents, the children and stepchildren of Madame Monet [...] Once the meal was finished we went back to the studio to have coffee, going through the blue living room where

The small blue livingroom

Monet's library was. It was there that Madame Monet, surrounded by her children and Monet's children, appeared to be in the full glow of a happy life; her bright eyes sparkled under her halo of powdered hair…"
Gustave Geffroy

The first studio which, before long,
became the living room-studio

THE FOLLOWING PAGE
A view of the garden
from a living room-studio window

Le Bassin d'Argenteuil 1872
CLAUDE MONET
Original: Musée d'Orsay, Paris

Nature morte au Melon vers 1872
CLAUDE MONET
Original: Fondation Calouste Gulbenkian, Lisbonne

Marine ou Le Voilier
CLAUDE MONET
Original: Musée Marmottan, Paris

L'Hôtel des Roches Noires à Trouville 1870
CLAUDE MONET
Original: Musée d'Orsay, Paris

"On the wall in his bathroom was Cezanne's Le Nègre Scipion, in blue pants; Monet, at the age of 18, by Deodat de Severac and in a corner, a little painting representing Monet in an African hunter's uniform; a watercolour of Boudin, La Pluie of Caillebotte as well as several other paintings and small landscapes in pastel by Monet. All the walls in his bedroom were covered with paintings. I counted eleven Cezanne and four Manet! By Renoir: the two portraits of Claude and of Madame Monet, Madame Monet lisant Le

The bedroom of Claude Monet

THE FOLLOWING PAGE
The bedroom of Alice Monet

Figaro, Une Algerienne, La Casbah, and two nude studies; a Degas, a few Jongkind; a Corot, and the portraits by Sargent of Monet, the one painting in his boat-studio and the other in his Basque beret with the painting of the Côte de Monaco as the background. And I forget some (not having taken notes except when Monet wasn't looking!). I did notice however that he didn't have one Gauguin or Van Gogh."

Paulette Howard-Johnston

"...the room was sunny, the lemon yellow walls were only decorated with Japanese prints; Monet told us that in the past he had bought them in packets for only a few francs in Holland. He assigned places to us [...] He poured drinks and watched how we helped ourselves to the dishes: "But you aren't eating." From his look we knew Monet expected our compliments and we gave them unsparingly." Jacques Salomon

Utamaro Kitagawa,
The Courtisan Karakoto from Choji-Ya

Hiroshige Utagawa,
Sudden Shower over Shin-Ohashi Bridge and Atake

Hokusai Katsushika,
Under the Wave off Kanagawa

"As regards lunch, Claude Monet's is marvelous. First of all, a few hors-d'oeuvres with the best Normand butter, succulent calf sweetbreads with spinach and then two chickens, all for five people: the first is roasted and no one will touch it, the second is extraordinary, made with black olives; and then a tart, a real delicacy, and fruit as beautiful as flowers. Monet has always loved being at the dining table." Rene Gimpel

*The garden of Monet counts
among his works, creating the charm
of an adaptation of nature
to the work of a painter of light.
An extension of the studio out of doors,
with palettes of colours profusely
spread all over for the gymnastics
of the eye, through appetites
of vibrations in which a feverish
retina waits for joys never appeased [...].
He didn't need to know how
he was making his garden. It's very certain that
he did as his eye successively ordered him,
responding to the invitations of each day,
for the satisfaction of his appetite for colour."*

Clemenceau

The Clos Normand

Monet's appreciation for gardens was long-standing. In a painting done by Manet during a visit to Argenteuil in 1874, titled *The Monet Family in the Garden*, Monet, in the background, is gardening and it is known that until the death of his other painter friend, Caillebotte, who also loved gardens, they exchanged gardening tools and tips. In the houses Monet lived in before Giverny, the gardens had already had many subjects: in Argenteuil, in the spring of 1872, he painted two times the same clump of lilacs, but in different lights, one in gray weather and the other in sunny weather. Even when he was in Paris, the public gardens sometimes served him as subjects, like the Tuileries and the Monceau park. It was in Giverny however that he was able to give the most of himself: he was at home, the money that he had lacked for a long time was finally coming in, and the land was vast and lent itself well. "All the money I earned went into my garden", he said. There, from a simple garden, he was going to progressively compose a space to paint.

When Monet acquired Giverny, a big orchard took up all the land in front of the house. A few clumps of bushes were scattered here and there and two long flowerbeds, one on each side of the central alley led to the entrance on the chemin du Roy, the road which ran along the property down below. Monet decided to make of this orchard a flower garden, a garden for the eyes, and without calling in a landscape architect: he loved natural gardens and simply hated anything artificial, like flowerbeds which were too regular, "rocks with waterfalls, giant mushrooms in cement placed at the foot of trees or on the lawn, columns, statues, tortured bushes, [...] perpetually trimmed into certain forms to be just cubes, cones, parasols and occasionally even French cockerels", as Jean-Pierre Hoschede, Alice's youngest son, noted with a touch of irony. Monet created a garden in front of the house, the Clos Normand, which had rather neat and straight pathways but which were overrun by a profusion of colourful flowers and bushes.

The main pathway was bordered with spruce and cypress trees. Monet didn't like either of them and decided to have them cut down. This started a family feud between the painter and Alice, who was opposed to the project. Monet

won on the question of the cypress trees and replaced them with metal arches which spanned the alley and which would soon be covered with climbing roses. As for the spruce trees, a compromise was reached: first of all, they were pruned and then cut halfway down, becoming simply trunks on which the roses would climb; when they ended up rotting, they were removed. Thus, with a beautiful archway of roses, the central pathway was bordered with climbing Nasturtium which spread out and didn't take long to overrun the gravel. The trimmed boxwood trees which bordered the pathway and the few clumps of bushes were also removed. Only two yew trees survived in front of the house. Monet had the benches and all the structures painted the same green he had chosen for the shutters and doors of the house.

On both sides of the central pathway, each part of the orchard was arranged differently. On one side, flower trees, cherry trees and Japanese apple trees replaced the old fruit trees, while clusters of irises and poppies planted here and there decorated the lawn. On the other side, the land was divided into several beds, each one having different flowers: gladiolas, larkspurs, phlox, asters, and big daisies. Each bed had a metal trellis which permitted the single clematises and the pink and white roses to climb. Most of the flowerbeds were surrounded with large borders of irises of all sorts.

Monet chose his plants himself, in France especially, and sometimes in England while his Japanese friends got peonies and irises for him. With his friends with green thumbs, like him, he exchanged advice, good addresses and plants. He consulted horticulture magazines and catalogues, visited their gardens and maintained good relations with many of them, in particular Georges Truffaut, who was often invited to the Monet's for a meal. He preferred single flowers to double ones. As in his painting, where he ended up eliminating blacks, he didn't like dark-coloured flowers. So that the garden would always have flowers, he skillfully mixed perennials and annuals.

If certain flowers were missing from Giverny, like sweet Williams, cannas, veronicas, and marigolds…, the abundance of the others that were found there was such that it would be impossible to name them all: poppies and single poppies, Nasturtium, sweet peas, snapdragons, lupin, peonies, narcissuses, gentians, tulips, asters, Japanese anemones, delphiniums, foxgloves, hollyhocks, larkspurs, clematises, irises, dahlias, aconites, plumbagos, rudbeckias, crocuses, gladiolas, bellflowers, phlox, China asters, single marigolds, and of course climbing roses and rose bushes. When the weather was very bad Monet grumbled and became disheartened: his garden was suffering and he couldn't work in it. "What sad weather and to add to it, the dejection of Monet faced with his garden wrecked by the downpour. He is distressed and he wants to take it out on everyone around him, which is really tiresome", wrote Alice to her daughter Germaine on 17 May 1907. When the flood of the century, that of 1910, caused the Seine to overflow and flood the gardens of Giverny, Monet broke down:

"The water is still rising; let's hope it's finally going to go down. […] In front of the pond there is one meter or more of water! It's distressing to see the poor pond with big brambles emerging alone; the rhododendrons and the azaleas are under water, the small bridges are floating, held in place by chains, and the big bridge risks being carried away. You see what state of mind Monet is in. He speaks only to groan", Alice wrote again to her daughter on 28 January 1910. When Monet was away from Giverny for his painting he continued to think about his garden and sent a lot of horticultural advice and recommendations to Alice.

"The weather has become much cooler and Eugene should be advised to cover the tiger-flowers and different plants that he knows. Especially with the moon, there has been fear of a frost. Also advise him that if there are sudden showers and hail (there was some here yesterday) to take the canvases down from the greenhouse." Monet to Alice

"Dear friend, be sure to come on Monday as planned; all my irises will be in bloom and later on would be too late. Here is the name of the Japanese plant that comes from Belgium: Crythrochaete. Try to speak to Mr. Godefroy about it and get me some information about its culture." Monet to Caillebotte

"I'll take this occasion to give you the address of the rose grower [...] and also the names of the rose-bushes that you noticed [...]: the one climbing the front of the house: Crimson Rambler and the one on a stem: Virago". Monet to the Bernheim-Jeune

"I'll see to it that these orders [for rosebushes] are delivered as soon as possible and I'll come to Yainville, bringing the plants I'm thinking of giving you [...] and will have everything planted in front of me".
Monet to Charlotte Lysès and Sacha Guitry

"We all worked in the garden; I dug, planted and weeded myself; in the evening the children watered. As the situation improved, I rested." Monet

"And the garden? Are there still flowers? I would love there still to be some chrysanthemums when I return. If there is a frost, make beautiful bouquets." Monet to Alice

"If one day I can see Claude Monet's garden, I feel sure that I shall see there a garden of even more tones and colours than flowers, one that is not so much a traditional flower garden but more a colourist garden so to speak, of flowers arranged in a way unlike nature, since they were planted so that only the *flowers of matching colors would bloom at the same time, harmonized in an infinite expanse of blue or pink, and that this intention of the painter, powerfully manifested, dematerialized, as it were, everything that wasn't colour."* Proust

"From a bare meadow, without one tree, but watered
by a babbling and winding branch of the river Epte,
he created a truly enchanting garden,
digging a large pond in the middle and around its edge planting
exotic trees and weeping-willows whose branches fall in long
tears on the bank, designing all around
paths whose arches of greenery,
in continually crossing and recrossing one another,
giving the illusion of a large park,
sowing on the pond a profusion
of thousands and thousands of water lilies,
whose rare and selected species colour
with all the colours of the prism,
from violet, red and orange to pink, lilac and mauve,
and lastly, planting on the river Epte,
at its outlet, one of those small rustic humped bridges,
as we see in the watercolors of the 18th century
and in the paintings of Jouy."

Thiébault-Sisson

The Water Garden

In 1893 Monet bought the land situated opposite the Clos Normand, on the other side of the road and the railroad tracks, beyond a tiny branch of the Epte, the Ru. Monet had the stream diverted and dug a pond almost 20 metres deep and a floodgate permitted renewing the water. In his letter to the prefect of the Eure asking for the authorization to make his garden, the painter's motives were clear: "It's only a question here of pleasure, of pleasing the eyes and having subjects to paint." In 1895 a wooden bridge spanned the pond. A few years later, in 1901, Monet purchased an adjoining piece of property which permitted him to extend the first pond towards the east. The new pond was then 60 metres long and 20 metres across at its widest point. The garden which surrounded the water lily pond was created entirely by Monet, who even had plants come from a horticulturist in the Lyon region who specialized in acquatic plants. The water lilies of different colours bloomed in the water while the irises, the arrowheads, the calthas or marsh marigolds, and the agapanthes bordered the slightly winding banks. Rhododendron, azalea, peony, rose and hydrangea bushes punctuate this water garden with patches of pink, white, red and garnet, while the willow and popular trees, regrouped at various intervals, shaded the pond. Protected by a little bamboo forest, the "Japanese" bridge, which spanned the pond soon collapsed under the abundant pale purple and white wisteria which hung on the metal structures. Two small boats, moored at the edge of the pond, permitted the painter and the gardeners to circulate on the edge of the water. Morning, afternoon and evening, Monet went for walks in his water garden, stopping for long moments in a precise place, continuing on and then stopping again.

Soon just the work of Monet, his children and a few day labourers wasn't enough to maintain the garden. Moreover, the cultivated plants in the greenhouse and under the numerous cold frames had to be taken care of. Having a head gardener became imperative. A very good friend of Monet and a lover of gardens too, Octave Mirbeau, found a very

competent gardener for him, Felix Breuil, the son of his father's gardener in the Orne. Assisted by four or five persons, he planted, dug, harrowed, sowed, cut, watered, weeded, and hoed season after season, making a marvelous garden of Giverny but always under the watchful eye of the painter, who multiplied his advice and instructions. In the water garden alone, one gardener was exclusively in charge of removing algae and duckweed and pulling off the water lily leaves that had become overrun. When Felix Breuil reached the age of retirement, another gardener, Lebret, took his place. He stayed there until his death during the Second World War.

For Monet, this water garden was an inexhaustible reserve of subjects and he did several series of paintings there which evolved with time. While the first series still leave a large place to the landscape itself, with the pond, the trees and the "Japanese" bridge, the following series reduced the landscape itself to a narrow strip in the upper part of the paintings, until it disappeared completely to the advantage of the water lilies and the reflections in the water. As the flowering of the water lilies lasted from the end of May until the end of September Monet worked on the subject for four months and then continued working on the paintings in his studio. Later on, with the *Big Decorations of Nympheas* done in his studio, the reflections prevailed in the end over the subject of the water lilies themselves.

"*Whereas you philosophically look for the intrinsic world, I simply put my efforts into the maximum of appearances, in close correlation with unknown realities.*" Monet

"I want to paint the air in which one finds the bridge, the house, the boat. The beauty of the air where they are, and this is nothing other than impossible." Monet

"*The pond, supplied by the River Epte, is flanked by willows of Babylon willows with golden branches. The beds and the banks are decorated with a masses of plants: heath-mould, ferns, kalmias, rhododendrons, azaleas and holly. The edges of the water are shaded on one side by densely grown rosebushes and the pond itself is planted with every known variety of water lilies. [...] A large bamboo plantation forms*

a dense woods. There are petasites with enormous leaves on the water's edge, thalictrums with jagged edges on the lawns, certain ferns with pink or white light downy flowers, wisteria... There are also tamarisks and long-stemmed roses and rosebushes are scattered over the whole area."

Georges Truffaut

"It took me time to understand my water lilies…I planted them without thinking of painting them… A landscape doesn't imbue you in a day… And then, all at once, I had the enchanting revelation of my pond. I picked up my palette. Since that time I've hardly had another model." Monet

"What has become of me, you can well imagine: I work and with difficulty because I'm losing my sight each day and I spend an enormous amount of time looking after my garden: it is a joy for me and with the beautiful days that we've had, I'm jubilant and in admiration of nature: with it, one doesn't have time to be bored." Monet to Gaston Bernheim-Jeune

"I sometimes went and sat on the bench from where Monet had seen so many things in the reflections of his water garden. My inexperienced eye needed perseverance to follow from afar the Master's brush to the ends of his revelations." Clemenceau

"I've already noticed, with everyone, that from the distance where Monet had to place himself to paint, the viewer only sees a tempest of madly mixed colours on the canvas. A few steps back and there, on the same panel, nature reconstructs and organizes itself miraculously, through the inextricable jumble of multicoloured

patches which disconcerted us at first sight. [...] How could Monet, who didn't move around, grasp, from the same view point, the decomposition and the recomposition of tones which permitted him to get the effect he was looking for?" Clemenceau

"I have painted many of these water lilies,
modifying my point of view each time,
renewing the subject depending on the season and as a result,
following the differences of the luminous effect
which bring about the changes.
The effect, for that matter, varies continuously.
What is essential in the subject is the mirror of water whose
aspect, at any moment, changes thanks
to the patches of sky reflected in it and which give it life and
movement. The cloud which passes over,
the breeze which freshens, the heavy shower
which threatens and falls, the wind which
blows and beats down suddenly,
the light which fades and reappears, so many causes,
imperceptible to the layman,
which transform the colour and change the ponds.

Monet to Thiebault-Sisson

The Studios

Monet worked at Giverny in three studios. The first, progressively transformed into a living room, was abandoned in 1899 for the second, a separate structure which was built on the west side of the house, on the site of the small old farm he had acquired. Almost square in shape and rather vast, the second studio benefited from abundant light thanks to a large surface of windows on the northern side, partly on the walls and partly on the roof; to the south, towards the greenhouses just down below and facing the garden, a gallery, at first open and later with windows, communicates with the studio. It was in this studio that Monet showed his paintings to his friends and as his success grew, to art dealers and amateurs. It isn't however open to visitors.

Finally, at the end of the property, Monet had a third studio built in 1916 on the site of an old house which had been a part of the henhouse for a long time. Already aged, he undertook very large formats, the future *Decorations of Nympheas*, which required a space both vast and light, allowing him to paint, no longer outdoors as he had done for so long, but in the studio. In order to get light directly from the sky, the roof was entirely glass, and a movable canopy was arranged to protect him from the sun. Central heating and electric fans softened the rigours of winter and tempered the heat of summer. The canvases, most of them six metres by two metres, were mounted on stretchers and were then fastened onto a support with wheels which made it possible to move them. In order to paint the upper part of the canvases without too much fatigue or acrobatics, Monet used a sort of large platform on which he could move around. Of course all the studies he had done for years outdoors helped him to paint these big decorative compositions. The day after the armistice of 11 November 1918 Monet proposed to his friend Clemenceau to offer two of them in celebration of the victory. Then, at the end of interminable discussions, he signed an act of donation to the State on 12 April 1922, according to which eight of them would be installed in two purpose-built, oval shaped rooms in the Orangerie Museum in the Tuileries Garden. It was only after his death on 17 May 1927 that the inauguration of the rooms took place; Monet had refused to deliver the paintings while he was alive.

Claude Monet Foundation

Thanks to the Reader's Digest and to the Lila Wallace-Reader's Digest Fund the farm, composed of three main parts of a building in ruin, situated just in front of the house and gardens of Claude Monet, and a piece of land, transformed into a parking lot embellished with trees and flowers, were acquired. The three main parts of the building were reconstructed with their original stones. In the building which runs alongside rue Claude-Monet the gardeners' general quarters, the head gardener's office and two bedrooms with a kitchen and bathroom for volunteers were installed. In the building to the right, thanks to certain donors, among which Mr. Laurance Rockefeller, a flower shop, a cafeteria and two apartments, for the important donors who come to Giverny from time to time, were installed. Finally, the big building at the back of the farmyard was completely restored by the Reader's Digest: since 1988, three well-equipped apartments and a big studio have thus been made available each year to three American artists that are chosen, as a way of rendering homage to the American donors, without whom Giverny wouldn't have become what it is today. Over the years the Foundation has collected 25 million dollars, from France but especially from the United States, which served to restore the domaine of Giverny. Henceforth Giverny, the most visited site in Normandy, welcomes from 450,000 to 500,000 visitors a year.

Fondation Claude Monet
84, rue Claude-Monet
27620 Giverny, France
tel.: 02 32 51 28 21
fax: 02 32 51 54 18
mail: contact@fondation-monet.com
site: www.fondation-monet.com
Curator: Mrs. Gerald Van der Kemp
General secretary: Mrs. Claudette Lindsey

The Foundation is open from
Tuesday through Sunday from 1 April to 31 October
from 9:30 am to 6:00 pm.
Open exceptionally on bank holiday Mondays
and all bank holidays

We wish to remind you that reservations
are not possible for individual visitors.
Our reservation service functions exclusively
for groups of a minimum of 20 or more people.
For information concerning groups
and group reservations only:
tel.: 02 32 51 90 31
fax: 02 32 51 91 32
mail: maguero@fondation-monet.com

Average length of time to visit the house
and the gardens : from 1 to 2 hours.
We regret to inform you that animals
are not allowed on the premises.

We wish to inform you that our offices remain open
for information and requests (group reservations...)
during the annual closure from 1 Novembre to 31 March
from 9:00 am to 5:00 pm
(except on Saturdays and Sundays and public holidays).

The Gift Shop
Our Gift Shop is located in the Nympheas studio near the garden.
It is open from 1 April to 31 October everyday
from 10: 00 am to 6: 00 pm, except Mondays.

The shop offers over 2,000 items including
an extensive selection of French and English books
on Claude Monet.

Access by train (SNCF): take the Paris-Rouen line,
departing from Paris, Saint Lazare station,
and descend at the station of Vernon.

Giverny's donors:

- Lila Wallace - Reader's Digest Fund
- The Academy of Beaux Arts
- The Departmental Council of the Eure
- The Society of Friends of Claude Monet
- The Society of the Friends
  of the Dallas Museum
- The Society of the Neuberger Museum
- S. E. and Mrs. Walter Annenberg
- Mr. and Mrs. David B. Arnold Jr.
- Mrs. Robert Arnold
- Mrs. Vincent Astor
- Mme Léon Bazin
- Mrs. Leigh Block
- Mrs. Alfred Bloomingdale
- Mr. Patrick Burns
- Mr. and Mrs. Edward Byron-Smith
- Mr. and Mrs. Gardiner Cowles
- Mrs. Ethel Woodward de Croisset
- Mrs. Allerton Cushman
- M. and Mme Pierre David-Weill
- M. and Mme Michel David-Weill
- The Ewind W.
  and Catherine M. Davis Foundation
- Mr. and Mrs. Frederick W. Davis
- M. and Mme Paul Desmarais
- John Deere and Company
- Mrs. Doris Duke
- Mr. and Mrs. Charles Durand-Ruel
- Mr. and Mrs. Thomas B. Evans Jr.
- Countess Alain d'Eudeville
- Mrs. Charles Engelhard Jr.
- Mrs. Frank Jay Gould
- The Florence J. Gould Foundation, Inc.
- Mr. Henry Ford II

- Mr. Alvin Fuller
- Mr. and Mrs. David Granger
- Mrs. Dolly Green
- Mr. and Mrs. Melville Hall
- Mrs. Ira Haupt
- Mr. and Mrs. Jack Heinz
- Mrs. James Hooker
- Mr. and Mrs. Philip Hulitar
- Mr. and Mrs. George F. Jewett, Jr.
- Mrs. Alistair J. Keith
- Mrs. Randolph Kidder
- Mrs. Eric Koenig
- Mr. and Mrs. David L. Kreeger
- Mme Yvonne Larsen
- Mr. and Mrs. Joseph Lauder
- Mr. and Mrs. Harding Lawrence
- Mr. and Mrs. Irvin Levy
- The Richard Lounsberry Foundation
- Mrs. Eugène McDermott
- Mr. and Mrs. Robert Magowan
- Mme Louis Marillonnet
- Mr. and Mrs. Harris Masterson
- Mr. and Mrs. Paul Mellon
- S. E. et Mme Walter Moreira y Salles
- Mrs. Charles Munn
- M. Stavros Niarchos
- Mr. George Ohrstrom
- Baron and Baroness Hubert von Pantz
- Mr. George Parker
- Mrs. Sandra Payson
- Mr. David Rockefeller
- Mr. Laurance Rockefeller
- Baron Edmond de Rothschild
- Mrs. Madeleine Russell

- M. Henri Samuel
- Mrs. Jay Simmons
- Mr. Garrick O. Stephenson
- Mr. and Mrs. Harold Stream
- Mr. and Mrs. David Schiff
- Marquise de Surian
- Mr. and Mrs. Vernon Taylor Jr.
- Miss Alice Tully
- M. and Mme Gerald Van der Kemp
- Mr. and Mrs. William Vincent
- Pierre J. Wertheimer Foundation
- Mr. and Mrs. William Wood-Prince
- Baroness van Zuylen
- Bergdorf Goodman
- Bloomingdale's
- Ceramich Caleca, S.r.l.
- Haviland and Parlon
- Marshall Field's
- Reed & Barton Corporation
- West Point-Pepperell, Inc.

**The following organization
is authorized to receive your donations:
Versailles Foundation**
Mme Gerald Van der Kemp, President
420, Lexington avenue
Graybar building
New York City N.Y. 10170

Editorial coordination: Denis Kilian, Director

Editorial follow-up: Karine Barou

Graphic conception: Juliane Cordes Atelier

Production: Pierre Kegels

Layout: Jérôme Poitte

Photo credits: Artlys/E. Burnier : p. 6, 22, 26, 27, 28-29, 33, 74, 76-77 ;
Artlys/A. Février : couverture, p. 1, 2-3, 6, 14, 16-17, 18, 20-21, 23,
24-25, 30-31, 34, 36-37, 40-41, 42-43, 44, 46, 47, 50, 51, 56-57, 60-61,
68, 72-73, 78 ; Artlys/A. De Kerland : p. 48-49, 68 ; Artlys/J. Girard : p. 6,
18, 19, 38-39, 45, 51, 52-53, 54, 58, 62-63, 64-65, 66-67, 68, 69, 70, 71;
RMN : p. 6, 32, 59 ; Louvre Bibliothèque et archives/RMN :
4ᵉ de couverture, p. 9 ; Louvre Bibliothèque et archives/RMN/Droits
réservés : p. 6, 10 ; RMN/R. Lambert : p. 32 ; RMN/T. Ollivier : p. 32.

Printing completed by Presses de Bretagne
may 2007
Legal deposit: may 2007
ISBN 2-85495-236-7
© Artlys, Versailles, 2004